Megan McDonald is the author of the popular series starring Judy Moody. She says, "Once, while I was visiting a class, the kids chanted, 'Stink! Stink! Stink!' as I entered the room. In that moment, I knew that Stink had to have a book of his own." Megan McDonald lives in California.

You can find out more about Megan McDonald and her books at **www.meganmcdonald.net**

Peter H. Reynolds is the illustrator of all the Judy Moody books. He says, "Stink reminds me of myself growing up: dealing with a sister prone to teasing and bossing around – and having to get creative in order to stand tall beside her." Peter H. Reynolds lives in Massachusetts.

You can find out more about Peter H. Reynolds and his art at **www.fablevision.com**

Stink-

O-PEDIA

SUPER
STINK-Y STUFF
FROM A TO Zzzzz

Megan McDonald   illustrated by Peter H. Reynolds

WALKER
BOOKS

A Anatomy of Stink

THIS IS ME!

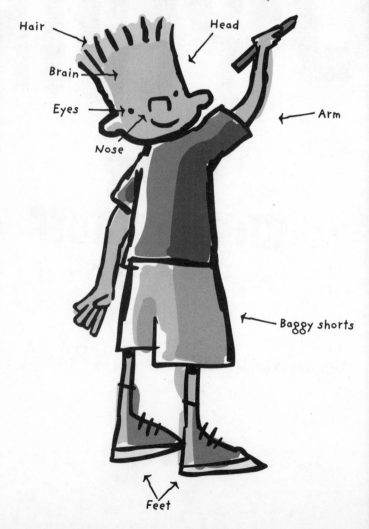

Hair

Head

Brain

Eyes

Nose

Arm

Baggy shorts

Feet

Anatomy of Stink A

HEIGHT:
112 centimetres (shrinks to 111.5 centimetres at night)

HAIR:
hair spikes, which help Stink look taller

NOSE:
super sniffer; can smell a corpse flower
a kilometre away

FEET:
live inside some of the world's worst super-
stinky sneakers

EYES:
fell asleep on the school bus and made him
miss his stop

ARMS:
got stuck in a PJ shirt; punched Webster
by mistake

HEAD:
size large, to fit genious brain

BRAIN:
full of encyclopedia facts, especially about
things beginning with the letter S

Astro (or Astro-NOT)

ASTROBLEME:
a circle left when a
meteorite crashes into Earth

ASTROCOMPASS:
finds true north in relation
to the stars and planets

A FEW FACTS ABOUT ASTRO, STINK'S FAVOURITE GUINEA PIG:

- has blue eyes
- has spiky hair like Stink
- found hiding out in the Great Wall of China
- took a ride on the Great Guinea Pig Express
- almost became snake food
- hitched a ride in Stink's backpack
- once wore Stink's undies

ASTROCYTE:
a star-shaped cell

FUR-EEKY!

Backpack Backbreakers **B**

Hidden compartment doubles as a Super Secret Survival Kit!

STINK NEVER LEAVES HOME WITHOUT:

- a guide to drawing comics
- a pocket edition of the S encyclopedia
- an old newt skin
- real (not-pirate) money
- a vial of anti-sister repellent
- his Toad Pee Club membership card
- a spare jawbreaker
- his James Madison friendship coin

Backpack Backbreakers

What's in your pack? Take a closer look...

PENS
A Parker ballpoint pen will produce
more than 8 kilometres of writing before
running out of ink.

PENCILS
The average pencil can be sharpened
seventeen times and write about 45,000
words.

ERASERS

One hundred years ago pencils did not have
erasers, because teachers thought that they
might encourage kids to make mistakes!

GLUE
The first patented glue was invented in
Britain in 1750. It was made from fish!

RULER
In 1994 scientists in Canada created the
world's smallest ruler. The teeny-tiny ruler
can measure stuff that is only one-sixtieth
of a human hair wide.

CRAYONS
A kid in the United States will wear down
730 crayons by the time he or she is ten.

Belly Button

While Stink is proud of his belly button, he thinks some things should remain PRIVATE. Judy, on the other hand, has no problem taking Stink's dried-up umbilical cord to school in a jar to show the entire third grade!

Know what omphaloskepsis is?
We've all done it. It's the art of zoning out, staring into space or contemplating one's navel.

ARE YOU AN INNIE OR AN OUTIE?

Some psychologists believe that your belly button holds a clue about the kind of person you are.

HORIZONTAL:	emotional
VERTICAL:	generous
OUTIE:	optimistic
INNIE:	gentle
OFF-CENTRE:	fun-loving
CIRCULAR:	calm, quiet

DID YOU KNOW?

Like fingerprints, no two belly buttons are alike.

Best Friends

WHAT TO KNOW ABOUT SOPHIE OF THE ELVES (AKA SOPHIE OF THE SMELLS):

- likes hobbits and elves
- won the Golden Clothes Peg Award for the smelliest sneakers
- once helped Stink make toilet water
- her favourite book starrs a brave mouse and an evil rat
- her favourite saying is "Fur-eeky!"
- one of her hopes for the future is to have a girl president

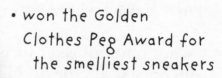

Best Friends

WHAT TO KNOW ABOUT WEBSTER
(AKA THE SMELLSTER):

- got punched by mistake during Stink's Attack of the PJs

- had his feelings hurt when Stink forgot about his birthday party

- his favourite book is **THE PURPLE SNAIL**

- got a Candy-Gram piñata from Stink

- his favourite saying is "Double gross!"

Birthdays and Birth (Oops!) Days

Jeep Baby! Stink made headlines when he was only a minute old, because he was born on the back seat of a Jeep on the way to the hospital.

STINK'S BIRTHDAY:
29 February, Leap Year!

JUDY'S BIRTHDAY:
1 April, April Fool's Day
(This is not an April Fool's joke!)

Other funny places where babies have been born:

- in a lift
- in a furniture shop
- in a taxi
- in a cinema
- in a Tube station
- at a petrol station
- at a restaurant
- at Disneyland

Brainiac = Brain + Maniac

Stink is a brainy, encyclopedia-reading maniac. His favourite volume? *S* (for "Stink"), of course!

The average adult human brain is 85 per cent water and weighs about 1.34 kilograms. The genius Albert Einstein had a pretty small brain, weighing in at 1.17 kilograms.

WANT A BETTER SCHOOL REPORT? EAT MORE BRAIN FOOD!

- Blueberries
- Strawberries
- Spinach
- Tofu
- Tuna fish
- Liver
- Peanut butter and banana sandwiches

DID YOU KNOW?

Peppermint has been known to increase brainwaves – just by its smell!

C Candyland

One of Stink's favourite hobbies is a trip to the Whistle Stop Sweet Shop for Tweezlers, Milk Dudes, Peanut Butter Yucks, Almost Joys and ... jawbreakers!

CELEBRATE SWEETS ALL YEAR LONG!

January

3rd – National Chocolate-Covered Cherry Day

26th – National Peanut Brittle Day

February

15th – National Gumdrop Day

March

24th – National Chocolate-Covered Raisin Day

April

12th – National Liquorice Day

22nd – National Jelly Bean Day

May

15th – National Chocolate Chip Day

PETER REYNOLDS'S FAVOURITE SWEET:
a tie between Reese's Peanut Butter Cups and Raisinets.

June is National Candy Month!
16th – Fudge Day

July
20th – National Lollipop Day
28th – National Milk Chocolate Day

August
30th – National Toasted Marshmallow Day

September
13th – International Chocolate Day
22nd – National White Chocolate Day

October
30th – National Candy Corn Day
31st – National Caramel Apple Day

November
7th – National Bittersweet Chocolate
with Almonds Day

December
7th – National Candyfloss Day
26th – National Candy Cane Day

MEGAN
McDONALD'S
FAVOURITE
SWEET:
a tie between
Reese's Peanut
Butter Cups
and Raisinets.
Same-same!

Comics

It's true. Stink Moody loves to read comics.

He likes to create his own comics even more.

What he likes most of all is imagining himself as **Stink, superhero!**

Comics

The Adventures of Stink
in Shrink Monster

BY STINK MOODY

The horrible Shrink Monster attacks the City of Moodyville!

ZAP!

EEEEK!

BEFORE

AFTER

ZAP!

Stink, the bravest (and shortest) kid in Moodyville, confronts the Shrink Monster!

GRRRRRR!

STOP!

ZAP

Huh?

Stink shrunk!

Max, fetch the Stink-Mobile.

Will Stink have enough time to invent an un-shrinker? Or will Stink be attending Molecule Primary School?

Good boy, Max.

Stink-Mobile

Comics

Comics

Corpse Flower

The world's biggest and worst-smelling flower is the titan arum, aka the corpse flower. Its odour can be so strong that the human nose can detect it more than half a kilometre away!

Stink's STINKY FACTS!

WHAT'S THE BIG STINK?

IT SMELLS LIKE ROADKILL AND LOOKS LIKE ROTTING MEAT. IT HAS SOME OF THE SAME CHEMICALS AS A DEAD BODY. IT ONLY BLOOMS FOR ABOUT THREE DAYS...

IT'S THE WORLD'S LARGEST, STINKIEST FLOWER— **THE CORPSE FLOWER!!**

UGH!

DID YOU KNOW?

On Stink's Reek Meter scale of 1–10, the corpse flower is an 11.

20

Duct Tape D

GOT TAPE?

Duct tape, a kid's best friend. Stink loves the stuff and once used it to build the Great Wall of China.

★ Springfield, Missouri, USA, is the duct tape capital of the world. There, more duct tape is sold per person than in any other place in the world.

★ The world's largest roll of duct tape weighs 295 kilograms and is 9,495 metres (or 9.5 kilometres) long! That's the same weight as six baby hippos and longer than 80 football pitches!

★ There's a new tape in town – the geckel! Researchers have come up with a tape so sticky, it works underwater. It was inspired by the gecko and the mussel, both of which have amazing "sticky" powers.

DID YOU KNOW?

Duct tape helped save the lives of the three astronauts on APOLLO 13.

E E is for _____

E is Stink's middle initial. Any guesses what it stands for?

Ebenezer?   Elwin?   Erving?

STINK E. MOODY

Eustace?   Eugene?

Visit www.stinkmoody.com and take a guess!

Encyclopedia

DID YOU KNOW?

Even encyclopedias sometimes make mistakes. Out of all printed English-language encyclopedias, Encyclopaedia Britannica has the fewest.

Stink loves to learn facts by reading the encyclopedia. His favourite is the *S* volume. If you want to find out what's in it, turn to page 86!

Nobody's Purfickt
See if you can find all of the spelling mistakes purposely printed in this book. Hint: there should only be twenty, counting the one on this page!

(Turn to page 139 for the answers.)

Eu-REEK-a!

Stink is known as The Nose. Whether it squeaks, reeks or freaks you out, he can smell it a mile away.

STINK'S REEK METER!

1 = not too smelly
10 = bring out the clothes peg!

- The tip of the stinkhorn fungus is covered with slime that flies love! To us, it would smell like rotting flesh.
  Reek Meter rating: 9

- The hairy blossom of the starfish flower from Africa attracts flies and maggots with its nauseating stench. Gag me with a spoon!
  Reek Meter rating: 7

- What smells like cat diarrhoea? *Sauromatum*, a flower that looks like a lizard! Don't give this one for Mother's Day.
  Reek Meter rating: 8.5

- In South East Asia there's a fruit called the durian that smells like rotten eggs. Airlines there had to enact a "no durian" rule because it was stinking up aeroplanes.
  Reek Meter rating: 11

F Fur & Fangs

A cat that makes toast? A chicken that plays the piano? One hundred and one escaped guinea pigs? You'll find them all at Stink's local pet shop, Fur & Fangs.

Fur & Fangs

MEET THE MOODY PETS

MOUSE

- is a cat
- likes mashed-up bananas
- knows how to make toast
- refuses to eat hair-covered prunes

JAWS

- It's a plant ... it's a pet ... it's a Venus flytrap! If you feed it raw minced meat, watch out — P.U.!

TOADY

- mascot of the Toad Pee Club
- almost had to wear undies for Show and Tell

NEWTON

- Class 2D's class pet
- state amphibian of "Newt" Hampshire
- took a big journey down the drane

GUESS WHO?

Fur & Fangs

MORE UNUSUAL PETS

🐾 Four-eyed fish can see above and below the water at the same time!

🐾 Potbellied pigs were first introduced to the United States from Asia in 1985. They are easy to train, curious and loving. They're smarter than the smartest dogs and love a good belly scratch.

🐾 If you hear a scream in the night, it's just your pet kinkajou. They're nocturnal, and their shrill call sounds like a blood-curdling scream.

DID YOU KNOW?

The Pilgrims kept skunks as pets!

Fur & Fangs

The wallaby is a mini kangaroo. They make affectionate, playful, mischievous pets. The wallaby is in the macropod family, which is named after the Latin word meaning "big foot".

In the 1970s pet rocks were a real hit. For £2, you could buy a rock painted with a tail and a face. The rock came with an owner's manual with hints on how to train your rock to sit, stay or roll over.

Stick insects are one of the most popular bugs to keep as pets. They hide by looking just like a branch of the plant they'll eat for lunch!

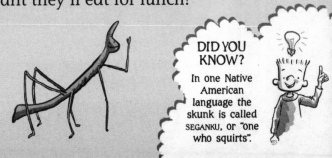

DID YOU KNOW?

In one Native American language the skunk is called SEGANKU, or "one who squirts".

G   Glow in the Dark

Stink's grandmother really knows what her grandson likes. When she buys Stink pyjamas, they're not just any pyjamas...

"These pyjamas are way better than the I ♥ TRUCKS ones I got last year," said Stink. "And the glow-in-the-dark part is kool-with-a-*k*!"

Excerpt from *Stink and the Incredible Super-Galactic Jawbreaker*

Glow in the Dark

Ever wondered how glow-in-the-dark stickers, stars or even glow-in-the-dark PJs work? They all contain phosphor, a substance that holds light, creating a soft green glow.

JELLYPIGS?
Scientists at National Taiwan University injected jellyfish protein into pig cells and came up with three green pigs that actually glow in the dark.

WHAT A MOUTHFUL!
Watch lightning strike — in your own mouth! Go into a dark room, bite down on a hard white wintergreen candy, and watch the sparks fly. Your teeth against the sweet make lite through friction. The big, fancy name for this is TRIBOLUMINESCENCE.

HARRY POTTER BY MUSHROOM LIGHT?
The ghost fungus, a mushroom found in southern Australia, emits a greenish light said to be bright enough to read by!

Guinea Pig Mania

It all began when Stink and his friends discovered three runaway guinea pigs in Webster's back garden. Next thing they knew, they were riding around Virginia with not three but 101 guinea pigs in need of good homes.

Guinea Pig Mania

Do you speak guinea pig? Here's a brief guide to help you translate what those little fur balls are saying:

WHEEK! *"I'm so excited!"* or *"I'm lost!"*

BURBLING *"Pet me"* or *"Yes, I like that."*

RUMBLING *"I'm the boss!"*

CHUTTING *"Run!"* or *"Help! I'm being chased!"*

CHATTERING *"Warning! Look out!"*

SQUEALING *"Danger, danger!"*

CHIRPING *"I'm so stressed!"*

WEE, WEE, WEE! *"I'm hungry! Feed me!"*

ARR! ARR! *"I'm lonely. Play with me."*

PURRING *"Let's explore; I feel curious."*

PTTP! *"I'm very happy!"*

RRRR! *"Ooh-la-la, I'm in the best mood ever!"*

Want to hear guinea pig speak? Try this:
www.mgpr.org/MGPR/Guinea%20Pig%20Sounds.htm

DID YOU KNOW?

Peter Reynolds had two pet guinea pigs when he was growing up. Their names were Willameena and Christina, and they liked to eat out of the bird feeder with the birds and the squirrels!

H Hic!

Hic! HIC! HIC!

HIC!

A pirate with hiccups? Scurvy Stink gets so excited about finding treasure that he could win the Hiccup Olympics.

Hiccup

Charles Osborne holds the world record for the longest attack of hiccups – sixty-eight years!

Hiccup

It's said that in that time, he hiccuped 430 million times.

HIC

HIC!

Hiccup

Lots of things can cause hiccups. One of the most common causes is eating too fast.

Hiccup

In the olden days hiccups were thought to be caused by elves.

DID YOU KNOW?

Scientists in France study tadpoles to learn about hiccups in humans.

HIC!

HIC!

HIC!

HIC!

32

HIC!

CAN YOU GUESS WHICH OF THE FOLLOWING ARE REAL CURES FOR HICCUPS?

HIC!

- ☐ Think of all the bald men you can.
- ☐ Close your eyes and picture a neon sign with the word THINK blinking off and on.
- ☐ Blow on your thumb.
- ☐ Scream.
- ☐ Say "pineapple".
- ☐ Talk non-stop for ten seconds.
- ☐ Count to twenty with your fingers in your ears.
- ☐ Rub your ear lobe.
- ☐ Chew gum.
- ☐ Balance a spoon on your nose.
- ☐ Smell a candle.
- ☐ Eat an ice lolly, dill pickle or marshmallow.

HIC!

(Turn to page 139 for the answer.)

33

Hugh Mongous and Other Huge Stuff

First it was short, shorter, shortest.
Then it was gigantic, super-colossal,
inter-galactic! Whether it's shortest,
tallest, stinkiest or grossest,
with Stink it's
always the
most-est!

Hugh Mongous

At Ocean Breeze Water Park in Virginia Beach, Stink and his friends get a close-up of Hugh Mongous, a giant (not real) gorilla dressed like a surfer. *Hang ten, dude!*

Q. *What's bigger than a football pitch, can be broken into 21,600 pieces, and took 777 people to put together?*

A. The world's largest jigsaw puzzle, built in Hong Kong.

DID YOU KNOW?

In his old age Benjamin Franklin couldn't reach the books on the top shelf, so he created the "long arm", a contraption with a grasping claw at the end of a long wooden pole.

Hugh Mongous

SEVERAL SUPER SUPERLATIVES

LONGEST WALL: the Great Wall of China, witch has almost four billion bricks and is more than 6,436 kilometres long.

LARGEST FROG: the African goliath frog, which measures 34.5 centimetres, nose to tail.

LARGEST JELLYFISH: the Arctic lion's mane jellyfish at 229 centimetres; tentacles, 36.6 metres.

HIGHEST JUMP BY A PIG: 70 centimetres.

MOST SOCKS WORN ON ONE FOOT: seventy.

TALLEST SANDCASTLE: 15 metres.

LARGEST UNDIES: 14.4 metres wide.

WORLD'S TALLEST (AND FASTEST!) ROLLER COASTER: Kingda Ka near Jackson, New Jersey, USA. Maximum height: 139 metres. Maximum speed: 206 kilometres per hour.

Hugh Mongous

LARGEST SANDWICH: 3,167 kilograms.

LOUDEST BURP: Paul Hunn of the UK holds the record for the world's loudest burp ever registered on a noise meter.

LARGEST PARTY OF PEOPLE DRESSED AS GORILLAS: 637. That's how many people joined the Great Gorilla Fun Run in London to raise money for the Dian Fossey Gorilla Fund.

LARGEST CARD TOWER: 422 centimetres tall (made of 162,000 cards).

LONGEST SKATEBOARD: 917 centimetres long, 25 centimetres wide and 5 centimetres thick.

I Idiom

"I am NOT an idiot!" said Judy.

"Id-i-*om*," said Stink. "It's what you call a funny saying. Like if you're in a bad mood, I could say you got out of bed on the wrong side."

Excerpt from *Stink and the Incredible Super-Galactic Jawbreaker*

Idiom

Can you match the correct idiom to the illustrations on the next three pages?

1. Feeling like a heel.
2. Making a mountain out of a molehill.
3. Costing an arm and a leg.
4. As cute as a bug's ear.
5. Sour grapes.

A.

B.

D.

C.

E.

(Turn to page 139 for the answers.)

41

Inventions

A RECIPE FOR ANTI-SISTER REPELLENT BY STINK E. MOODY

To a jar of toilet water, add dash of smelly stuff. Voilà! Judy-Moody-Be-Gone! It's almost as good as bug spray

Inventions (By real kids like you!)

- **LOUIS BRAILLE** was only fifteen when he invented a way for the blind to read and rite by using raised dots.

- **CHESTER GREENWOOD** was seventeen when he invented earmuffs in 1873.

- **GEORGE NISSEN**, at the age of sixteen, invented the trampoline out of old junk.

- At the age of eleven, **FRANK EPPERSON** left a stir stick in his soda and it froze. Eureka! The first Epsicle. His kids later changed the name to Popsicle.

- In 1922 **RALPH SAMUELSON** invented waterskiing. He made his first pair of waterskis out of slats from barrels at the age of eighteen.

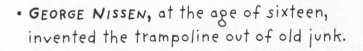

DID YOU KNOW?

When Peter Reynolds was Stink's age, he invented a time machine. But it was only big enough for a mouse. Who knows if the time machine worked? When the mouse got back, all it said was "Squeak!"

J James

"How'd you get the name Stink, anyway?" asked Sophie of the Elves.

"HER," said Stink, pointing at Judy.

"I'll tell it! I'll tell it!" Judy said. "One day, when Stink was a baby, Dad was changing Stink's dirty nappy..."

"Eee-yew!" said Webster, pinching his nose.

"Anyway, it was really stinky. So I started singing this song I'd learned at nursery."

"Don't sing it!" said Stink, covering his ears.

"Sing it!" said Webster and Sophie.

"It sounds like 'Old McDonald Had a Farm':

> *My little brother smells so bad,*
> *Stinky, stinky poo!*

Ever since then, we've called him Stinky Poo," said Judy.

"Then one day, it got shortened to just plain Stink," said Stink.

Excerpt from *Stink and the World's Worst Super-Stinky Sneakers*

Jawbreakers

Stink likes sweets. He likes them even more when they're *FREE*.

- A jawbreaker starts with one tiny grain of sugar. The sugar is whirled around and around until it snowballs to the right size.

- It would take an average-size frog approximately two years to digest the world's largest jawbreaker.

OTHER NAMES FOR JAWBREAKERS:

GOBSTOPPER   ANISEED BALL

GRAPESHOT   JAW BUSTERS

FIREBALL   LEMONHEAD

Jawbreakers

Judy

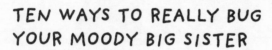

It's not the way Stink would have planned it, but in the Moody family Judy is the oldest (and tallest) kid, and Stink is the youngest (and shortest).

TEN WAYS TO REALLY BUG YOUR MOODY BIG SISTER

1. Hide your smelliest sneakers under her bed.

2. Repeat everything she says.

3. Have a staring competition without telling her.

4. Talk by moving your lips without making any sound.

5. Take a picture of her while she's sleeping, then show her friends.

6. Steal her mood ring (or dessert!) when she's not looking.

7. Pretend to wipe spit off your face while she's talking.

8. Sing "Happy Birthday to You" when it's not her birthday.

9. Tap a pencil on the table while she's trying to do her homework.

10. Make her give you a pound to stop bugging her!

Ka-Ching! K

Stink made fifty cents a bag selling moon dust. He tried to charge a quarter just for telling Rocky what Judy said when they had been in a fight. He even got a five-dollar gift voucher just for being short. Stink is always on the lookout for a way to make a buck.

Hand over that clam!

In the USA, where Stink lives, they use dollars.

It costs 4.2 cents to make a dollar bill.

NICKNAMES FOR A ONE-DOLLAR BILL:

CLAM   BUCK   SMACKEROO

APER   SINGLE

BONE   ONE

GREENBACK   BILL   DEAD PRESIDENT

DID YU KNOW?

Every day, 16,650,000 one-dollar bills are printed. Most of these replace worn-out money, which gets shredded.

Karate

Look out. When Stink starts karate-chopping everything from pencils to rulers, it could spell trubble.

★ Karate is thousands of years old. Because weapons were banned in Okinawa for many years, the Japanese learned hand-fighting techniques.

★ The word KARATE comes from two Japanese characters. KARA means "empty" and TE means "hand".

DID
YOU
KNOW?

The most concrete blocks busted by hand in one minute is 90.

★ The bone in your hand is forty times stronger than concrete. Still, it takes years for karate experts to learn to break a piece of wood with their hand.

Letters and Letter Writing L

Greetings, Salutations, PS
Stink learns all about writing letters in Mrs D.'s class. There's no stopping the mighty pen of Stink E. Moody.

The oldest message in a bottle spent 92 years and 229 days at sea! The bottle, numbered 423B, was recovered by UK fisherman Mark Anderson on 10 December 2006.

DID YOU KNOW?

In Canada, Santa has his own postcode: HOH OHO.

Letters and Letter Writing

"THE MAIL MUST GO THROUGH"

In 1861 the pony express had to speed President Lincoln's inaugural address from St Joseph, Missouri, USA, to Sacramento, California. Rider "Pony Bob" was shot in the arm and through the jaw by two arrows, but he kept on riding. He rode 193 kilometres in eight hours, stopping for only a few minutes to bandage his wounds.

DID YOU KNOW?

The pony express delivered 34,753 letters. Letters were written on lightweight paper and wrapped in oiled silk to protect them from the weather.

Letters and Letter Writing

A DANGEROUS BUSINESS...

WANTED

YOUNG, SKINNY, WIRY FELLOWS NOT OVER 18. MUST BE EXPERT RIDERS, WILLING TO RISK DEATH DAILY.

ORPHANS PREFERRED.

PONY EXPRESS

DID YOU KNOW?

Megan McDonald once had a job where she got to transcribe old letters written by George Washington himself. His writing sure was hard to read!

Letters and Letter Writing

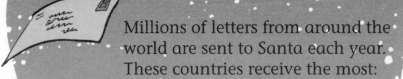

Millions of letters from around the world are sent to Santa each year. These countries receive the most:

FRANCE	1.22 million
CANADA	1.06 million
US	1 million
UK	750,000
GERMANY	500,000

NORTH POLE, ALASKA, USA, receives more than 120,000 letters to Santa per year.

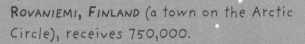

ROVANIEMI, FINLAND (a town on the Arctic Circle), receives 750,000.

In ROVANIEMI elves are needed to help Santa answer all the letters. But you have to study at the Elf Academy in order to be one of Santa's helpers.

Other duties include wrapping presents, making fires in the snow and knowing the names of the local wildlife.

Madison, James M

Stink's favourite president, James Madison, is the Shortest President Ever (but still a Big Cheese).

James Madison = 163 centimetres
James "Stink" Moody = 112 centimetres

Do the maths! How much shorter is Stink Moody than James Madison?

(Turn to page 140 for the answer.)

James Madison

DID YOU KNOW?

James Madison liked ice cream and had a pet parrot.

James Madison was only twenty-five years old when he started to write the US Constitution. To make himself look older, he always wore black and put white powder in his hair.

Moon Rocks

Stink is loony for the moon and finds space far out. He even owns his very own moon rock. Well, he used to own his very own moon rock...

SMASH!

"It's not a moon rock any more!" cried Stink.

"Look at it this way, Stink," said Judy. "Now you have something better than a moon rock."

"What could be better than a moon rock?" asked Stink.

"Lots and lots of moon dust."

Excerpt from *Judy Moody*

DID YOU KNOW?

Moon dust is about 50 per cent silicon dioxide glass, created when meteorites hit the moon.

Moon Rocks

★ The National Cathedral in Washington DC, USA, has a special stained-glass window that contains piece no. 230, a tiny bit of rock brought back from the moon by APOLLO 11.

★ 2,415 moon roks were collected by US Apollo missions.

★ A new mineral found on the moon was named armalcolite for the three astronauts on APOLLO 11. Can you name those three?

(Turn to page 140 for the answer.)

DID YOU KNOW?

The oldest rock found so far on Earth is 3.8 billion years old. The oldest moon rock recovered so far is 4.5 billion years old.

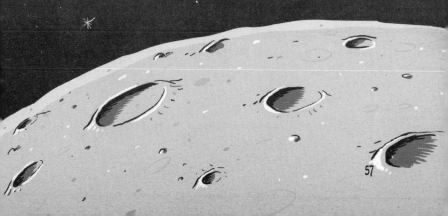

Mouse

A cat named Mouse? Only at the Moodys' house! And like the rest of the family, Mouse has her moods.

MOUSE MOOD METER

HAPPY CAT
She's lying on her belly, eyes half closed, and purring.

MAD CAT
She's puffed up and arching her back, flicking her tail from side to side.

SCAREDY-CAT
Her ears are flattened, she's crouching and she avoids eye contact.

WORRY CAT
She's flicking her tongue and twitching her ears back and forth.

Museums

Stink loves museums almost as much as he loves encyclopedias.

HIS FAVES

- The Gross-Me-Out exhibition at the science museum.

- The Isle of Wight Museum, home of the world's oldest ham.

Museums

CHECK OUT THESE OTHER WAY-COOL, FOR-REAL MUSEUMS:

- THE ALIMENTARIUM FOOD MUSEUM, Vevey, Switzerland, has a 4,200-year-old cake.

- LUNCH BOX MUSEUM, Columbus, Georgia, USA

- BANANA MUSEUM, Hesperia, California, USA
  Home of the petrified banana and a banana phone.

- INTERNATIONAL UFO MUSEUM, Roswell, New Mexico, USA
  Flying saucer? Alien? Weather balloon? Find out about the mysterious crash-landing near Roswell in July 1947.

- COCKROACH HALL OF FAME, Plano, Texas, USA

- MUSEUM OF DIRT, Boston, Massachusetts, USA
  Dirt from Antarctica, not to mention fluff donated by author Dave Barry.

- LEILA'S HAIR MUSEUM, Independence, Missouri, USA
  More than 2,000 objects made of human hair.

- MUSÉE DES ÉGOUTS DE PARIS, PARIS, France
  Tour the sewers of Paris. P.U.!

DID YOU KNOW?

The Burnt Food Museum in Arlington, Massachusetts, USA, is temporarily closed due to fire damage!

Newts N

When Stink brought home his classroom pet, Newton, he learned all there was to know about way-not-boring newts in *Newtsweek* magazine.

DID YOU KNOW?

If a newt loses an eye, it can grow a new one! The same goes for losing a limb, the heart, part of the intestine, or a jaw.

Newts

LIFE CYCLE OF A NEWT

Newt eggs are
laid in the water.

When the young newts
hatch, they can
breathe only
with gills, so
they spend the
first part of their
lives in the water.

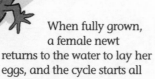

When fully grown,
a female newt
returns to the water to lay her
eggs, and the cycle starts all
over again.

Some newts leave the water for
land at this time and are known
as red efts. They are red-orange at
this stage but turn green
as they mature over a
two- to three-year period.

As the newts grow,
they develop lungs
for breathing air.

Nose

The human nose can detect 10,000 different smells. Stink was born with a very special nose, a super sniffer.

- Most people think birds can't smell. But in fact, they use smells to make a "map" of where to fly.

- An elephant's trunk can smell water from nearly 5 kilometres away.

- Your nose is at its peak — can smell the most smells — when you are ten years old.

EDWARDO AND HIS NOSE MAXIMA

DO YOU HAVE RHINOTILLEXOMANIA?

It's not scurvy.

It doesn't mean you're crazy for rhinos.

It means you're bogey-crazy —
can't stop picking your nose.

DID YOU KNOW?

Your nose produces about half a litre of mucus in one day! That's snot even funny!

63

O Optical Illusions

Sometimes Stink feels like a shrimp, a shortcake, a *stunt*ed man. Stink's sister, Judy, tells him that wearing clothes with up and down stripes will give the *illusion* that he is taller than he really is. Check out these other tricks you can play on your eyes.

Are these staggered black and white stripes exactly the same width from end to end? Get out your ruler and measure!

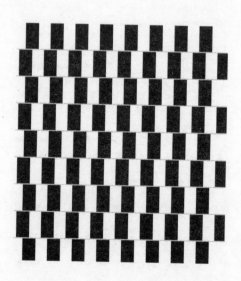

Optical Illusions

Now try looking at these black and white stripes. Are they straight or curved?

Look at these two flowers. Which centre spot is bigger, the one in the flower on the left or the one in the flower on the right? Are you sure?

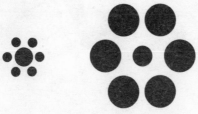

(Turn to page 140 for the answers.)

P Pirates

Scurvy Stink and Mad Molly O'Maggot (Judy Moody) pick up some pirate rules and lingo as they search for treasure on Ocracoke Island, where the real Pirate Blackbeard once sailed the seas and swung his hammock.

DID YOU KNOW?
19 September is International Talk Like a Pirate Day!

66

Pirates

SCURVY STINK. MAD MOLLY O'MAGGOT.
Pick a word from each column to
create yer own fearsome name!

Mad	Bones	Archibald
Deadeye	Badfish	Pete
Cutthroat	Ratfink	Pegs
Scurvy	Catfish	John
Bilge	Keelhaul	Obadiah
Black	Coal	Alligator
Sneaky	Gunwales	Baldhead
Jolly	Dirtyfoot	Canker
Slimy	Swordfish	Vulture
Blimey	Buccaneer	Albatross
Iron	Bloody	Ivan
Voodoo	Yardarm	McPhee
Bloody	Crow's Nest	Brigadoon
Grimy	Terrible	Dublin
Dread	Cankersore	Vane
Skylarking	Frosty	Funkhole

Pirates

TIPS FOR TALKING LIKE A PIRATE

Always say "ye" for "you" and "me" for "my". Throw in lots of "Ahoy!" and "Arrr!" The following list will also help you along.

"AHOY!" . . . . "Hello, there!"

"ARRRRRR!" . . . . expression of glee

"AVAST!" . . . . "Hey!" or "Who goes there?"

"BILGE!" . . . . "You're nuts!" or "That's crazy!"

"BLIMEY!" . . . . expression of surprise

BOOTY. . . . . loot or money

BUCKO . . . . friend or pal

DAVY JONES'S LOCKER . . . . bottom of the see

DOG . . . . insult, as in "You dog!"

DOUBLOON . . . . a Spanish gold coin

FEED THE FISH . . . . pirate punishment

GRUB . . . . food, eats

Pirates

HEAD . . . . the toilet, the loo

JOLLY ROGER . . . . pirate flag; means "You should surrender!"

LANDLUBBER . . . . non-sailor

ME HEARTIES . . . . pirate captain's crew

MATEY . . . . person or friend

PIECE OF EIGHT . . . . a Spanish silver coin

SCURVY . . . . (1) a disease among sailors caused by lack of vitamin C
. . . . (2) a put-down, as in "Ye scurvy dog!"

SEA DOG . . . . an experienced seaman

"SHIVER ME TIMBERS!" . . . expression of surprise or strong emotion

WALKING THE PLANK . . . . a made-up pirate punishment

"YO-HO-HO!" . . . . nobody knows what this means, but pirates sure say it a lot.

Pluto

Stink is hopping mad when he learns that Pluto has been demoted from a Planet to a Planet Jr. He's got to learn more about Pluto if he's going to save it.

Pluto, which was considered to be the ninth planet for seventy-five years, failed a grade in 2006 and is now only a dwarf planet. Its new name is not even a Greek god of the underworld. It's a number: 134340.

How do you remember the order of the planets from the sun? This trick used to work wonders:

My Very Educated Mother Just Served Us Nine Pizzas.

Mercury, Venus,
Earth, Mars,
Jupiter, Saturn,
Uranus, Neptune,
Pluto.

Now try this:

My Very Educated Mother Just Served Us Nachos.

Mercury, Venus, Earth, Mars, Jupiter, Saturn, Uranus, Neptune, Pluto.

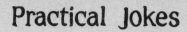

Practical Jokes

Fake hand in the toilet. Pickle-flavoured gum. Moon rock. Stink and Judy are always playing tricks on each other. Here are a few to try on your friends and family:

- ☺ Fill a tray of ice cubes with water, dropping a plastic ant, fly or bug into each section before freezing. Then drop one into someone's lemonade!

- ☺ Replace the filling in any creme-filled biscuit with toothpaste.

- ☺ Pour spicy sauce on your friend's slice of pizza when he or she is not looking.

- ☺ When your dad goes to sit down, rip a piece of fabric so he'll think he's split his trosers.

Practical Jokes

⟳ Superglue 20p to the pavement outside your house. Laugh yourself silly when somebody tries to pick it up.

Professional Smeller

NOSE JOB!

Stink wants to put his super sniffer to work when he grows up, and become a professional smeller.

What do YOU want to be? Not sure? Turn the page for a few ideas.

DID YOU KNOW?

Professional pig-poop sniffers row, row, row their boats out into the middle of a pond of pig poop to take a whiff and a sample. They test it to measure how much methane is produced.

Professional Smeller

YOU COULD GROW UP TO BE A:

HAIR-SIMULATION SUPERVISOR
Your job, should you choose to accept it, is to make 3D hair for animated cartoons! Way cool!

BANANA GASSER
WHAT? Yep, you too can spray bananas with a gas that speeds up ripening.

SNAKE MILKER
Animal care experts are hired to extract venom from poisonous snakes by "milking" the reptiles' fangs. The venom is then used in serums that treat snake bites.

BANK ROBBER
Hack into computers at banks to help banks learn just how easy or hard it is. That's an order!

BUBBLE POPPER
Get a job testing bubble wrap. It's a blast!

Professional Smeller

MORE REAL-LIFE JOBS
TO THINK ABOUT:

HAUNTED-HOUSE ACTOR

JAM-DOUGHNUT FILLER

UFO TRACKER

MUSHROOM HUNTER

SOCK TURNER

HUMAN CANNONBALL

CHEESE IMPERSONATOR

GLUE CHECKER

PROFESSIONAL SLEEPER

OSTRICH BABYSITTER

GUM BUSTER

(WHO DO YOU THINK REMOVES ALL
THAT GUM FROM UNDER STUFF?)

FORTUNE-COOKIE WRITER

Q Q & A

Test your Stink IQ here:

1. How many freee jawbreakers did Stink get from the jawbreaker company?

2. What award did Stink want to win for the World's Worst Smelly Sneaker Contest?

3. What book was Stink reading for Pyjama Day?

4. What is Stink's name in Hawaiian?

5. What is the name of Stink's postman?

6. What number did Stink wear for Presidents' Day and why?

7. Why was Stink afraid to go to the nurse's office at school?

8. What place did Stink choose to visit on his way to Virginia Beach in the Guinea Pig Express?

SUPER-INTELLIGENT ALL-TIME BONUS QUESTION

Q: What is the name of Stink's two-metre-long stuffed-animal snake?

(Turn to page 140 for the answers.)

Quill Pen

Before there were ballpoint pens, there were quill pens, made from large bird feathers. Goose feathers were the most popular.

DID YOU KNOW?

President Thomas Jefferson wrote almost 20,000 letters in his lifetime. That's a lot of quill pens!

Quill Pen

★ The Bible, the Magna Carta, the Declaration of Independence, the Emancipation Proclamation and the US Constitution were all penned using a quill.

★ The US Constitution was written with a quill by Jacob Shallus, a Pennsylvania clerk, for a fee of $30 or £18 ($325.29 or £199 in today's money).

★ At the National Archives, pages one and four of the US Constitution are on display in a bulletproof case. The entire document is displayed once a year on 17 September, the anniversary of the day the framers signed the document.

DID YOU KNOW?

The US Supreme Court still uses 1,200 quills a year! This goes back to a tradition that began in 1801.

R Rescue Me!

Q: *How many guinea pigs does it take to fill a camper van named Squeals on Wheels?*

A: 101, rescued by Stink!

OTHER FAMOUS RESCUES

- On 15 April 1912 the ship CARPATHIA rescued 705 TITANIC survivors from their lifeboats in the icy waters of the North Atlantic.

- Faith, a four-year-old rottweiler in Richland, Washington, USA, speed-dialled 999 on the phone when her owner fell and was knocked unconscious.

- In February 1925 a deadly diphtheria epidemic was wiping out the young people of Nome, Alaska, USA. The only medicine that could stop the epidemic was over 1,000 kilometres away. A dog named Balto led a team of sleigh dogs in a life or death race to get the serum in time to save the children. That famous run led to a yearly dog-sleigh race called the Iditarod.

83

Rodents

A funny bone is not a bone.
A prairie dog is not a dog.
And a guinea pig is not a pig –
it's a rodent.

Excerpt from *Stink and the Great Guinea Pig Express*

- There are 2,277 species of rodents in the world. These species can be found on all continents except Antarctica.

- Forty per cent of all mammals are rodents. They have sharp incisors (teeth) and have been around for 65 million years.

Rodents

🐾 The giant beaver, the giant dormouse and the Flores giant rat are just a few of the prehistoric rodents that once scurried and scrabbled across the earth.

🐾 A capybara is the largest living rodent. It weighs 45 kilograms, the same wait as President James Madison!

S Secret Codes

Stink and his sister, Judy, are code-busters. While on an island treasure hunt, they have to crack riddles and secret codes to win pirate booty and a ride on a pirate ship. Take a crack at these super-secret codes:

THE INCHWORM CODE

1. Lay a ruler on a piece of blank paper.

2. Think of your secret message.

3. Beginning with the first letter of your message, write each letter of your message a centimetre apart (at the centimetre marks on the ruler).

4. Lift up the ruler and fill in each gap with random letters to confuse counterspies.

 Make sure you tell your friend about on the ruler trick so that he or she can decode your message with a ruler.

Secret Codes

A simpler version of the Inchworm
Code is to insert a single random
letter between each letter in your
message as you write it, like this:

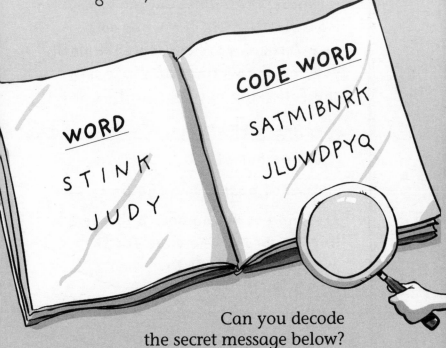

CODE WORD

SATMIBNRK

JLUWDPYQ

WORD

STINK

JUDY

Can you decode
the secret message below?

SPKOIMNRKES RMUBLTEX

(Turn to page 140 for the answer.)

Secret Codes

THE BOOKWORM CODE

This secret code uses words borrowed from a book and turns them into numbers. Pretend you want to write a message that has the word GOLD in it. Flip through your chosen book until you find the word GOLD. Write down the following numbers, in this order:

a. page number

b. line number

c. word position in the line

Pretend you found GOLD on page 23, line 4, word 9. The code for the word GOLD would then be **23 4 9.**

Make sure you tell your friend which book he or she needs to have handy in order to decode your message.

Secret Codes

Decode the following secret message using the book STINK AND THE WORLD'S WORST SUPER-STINKY SNEAKERS:

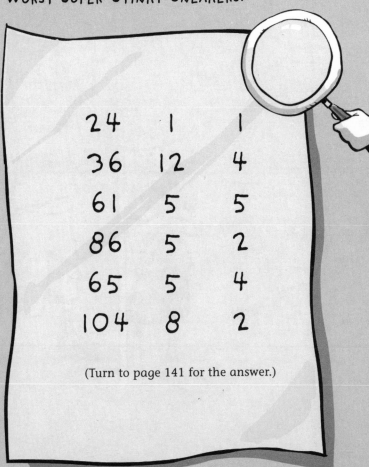

24	1	1
36	12	4
61	5	5
86	5	2
65	5	4
104	8	2

(Turn to page 141 for the answer.)

Short, Shorter, Shortest!

Stink is the shortest person in
the Moody family. Imagine
his surprise one evening
when he discovered that,
instead of growing that
day, he'd shrunk! Chances
are that you have too.
Want to find out? Here's how:

Get someone to measure your height first thing
in the morning, then again last thing at night.

Shrink Shrank Shrunk

By the end of the day, you're likely to be a little
shorter than you were first thing in the morning.

Why? During the day, gravity pulls down on
your spine, which squeezes out some of the
water between the spinal discs. This water is
replaced as you sleep each night. The water
works as a cushion between the discs.

**DID
YOU
KNOW?**

The shortest
man ever
was Gul
Mohammed
of India,
who was
only 56
centimetres
tall.

Short, Shorter, Shortest!

MORE WAY-COOL SHORT STUFF!

★ In the Galápagos Islands iguanas actually shrink in length by as much as 20 per cent when there's not enough red and green algae to eat. That's like Shaquille O'Neal shrinking from his 216-centimetre height down to 173 centimetres. Even the iguana's bones shrink, not just their cartilage. When the algae return, the iguanas grow again.

★ In the old days high heels became popular among women and men. This fad started with vertically challenged royalty so they could look taller.

★ During the French Revolution, a man named Richebourg became the shortest spy ever. He was just 58 centimetres tall and carried secret messages in and out of Paris while disguised as a baby carried by his "nurse".

DID YOU KNOW?

Peter Reynolds was vertically challenged (aka short!) when he was Stink's age. One day he met a girl named Spider who was short too, and they became instant best friends.

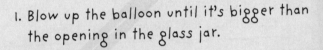

THE INCREDIBLE SHRINKING BALLOON

You will need:
- 1 balloon
- 1 glass jar
- 1 bowl of iced water

1. Blow up the balloon until it's bigger than the opening in the glass jar.

2. Try to put the balloon into the jar. Won't fit? Place the balloon in the bowl of iced water and leave it there for a minute or so.

3. Try again. This time the balloon should fit through the mouth of the glass jar.

How did that happen? While hot air expands, cold air contracts or shrinks. When the air inside the balloon was cooled, the balloon shrank, enabling it to fit through the mouth of the jar. Now, that's cool!

Skeletons

Stink does not like visiting the school nurse's office because of Mr DryBones, the clickety-clackety skeleton hanging in the corner. Creepy!

> "Wait a minute! Stink! I've got it! I know what you have!"
> "What?" asked Stink.
> "Skeleton-itis!" said Judy. "Fear-of-Skeletons disease."
>
> Excerpt from *Judy Moody: The Doctor Is In!*

DID YOU KNOW?

A human has 206 bones. But when you're born, you have 300. As you grow up, some bones fuse together.

◎ The blue whale skeleton is the largest museum skeleton and was found in New Zealand.

◎ The world's largest snake skeleton is that of a 670-centimetre-long reticulated python at the Cornell University Museum of Vertebrates, USA.

◎ At 13 metres long, Sue, on display at Chicago's Field Museum of Natural History in the USA, is the largest T. rex skeleton ever.

Skinks

Stink loves to read about the skink (rhymes with *Stink*!) – a small cone-headed lizard with shiny scales. Stink gets the skinny on skinks from – what else? – the *S* volume of the encyclopedia.

◎ Skinks can see with their eyes closed! (They have a see-through scale on the lower eyelid.)

◎ The Australian blue-tongued pygmy skink was thought to be extinct until – EUREKA! – in 1992 one was discovered in the belly of a snake.

◎ When a skink is being chased, it can lose its tail to trick the predator. No worries! It can grow a new one.

◎ ACHOO! Skinks sneeze a lot. It's how they clear dirt from their nostrilz.

DID YOU KNOW?

The Solomon Islands giant skink can grow to 71 cm long. That's a lot of skink!

Slime

Gross me out! Stink-o! Skunksville!
Where there's smelly stuff, slime cannot
be far behind.

- Hippos don't sweat; they slime!
  Hippo slime stops hippos getting
  sunburned and also kills germs! It
  starts out clear, turns orange-red,
  then turns brown!

- Slime eels are covered head to tail
  in gross, yucky, mucous-y slime!
  Scientists call them hagfish or slime
  hags. When a predator gets too close,
  a slime eel throws out a stream of
  slime to "jelly" the enemy.

Slime

MAKE YOUR OWN GOOP, GAK, GUNK

You'll need:

31.5 g cornflour   113 g white glue

1/2 teaspoon borax   60 ml warm water

food colouring

1. Sift cornflour into a big bowl.

2. Add glue and stir (and stir and stir!).

3. In a second bowl, mix the warm water

   with the borax and food colouring.

4. Now add this mixture to the first bowl.

5. Stir well, even after the slime has formed.

   You can add several drops of glow-in-the-dark

   paint to make your slime glow.

DID YOU KNOW?

Slugs use their slime to travel upside bown. Slugs have been caught eating their own slime! GROSS!

Snowflakes

Stink wants only one thing for Christmas. One teeny-tiny thing. One puny word. Hardly even a present. And that one thing is ... SNOW! But it hasn't snowed on Christmas Day in Virginia for about a hundred years.

DID YOU KNOW?

Some snow is actually red, green, blue or black. But snow crystals reflect the full spectrum of light, which makes us see snow as white.

Wilson A. "Snowflake" Bentley was the first man to photograph snowflakes and crystals. He made a special microscope camera that took pictures of these snow formations.

snowflake chart

 Sheath

 Simple Prism

 Solid Column

 Cup

 Simple Star

 Arrowhead Twins

 Hexagonal Plate

 Hollow Column

 Radiating Stinks

 12-Branched Star

 Crossed Needles

 Stellar Plate

 Capped Column

 Bullet Rosette

 Stellar Dendrite

 Simple Needle

 Sectored Plate

 Twin Columns

 Isolated Bullet

 Radiating Dendrite

Superheroes

Save me, Mr Insecto Magnetic Doomstopper!

When he's not reading the encyclopedia or rounding up guinea pigs, Stink is out saving the world as Newt Boy!

MAKE UP YOUR OWN SUPERHERO!
(CHOOSE ONE WORD FROM EACH COLUMN)

Cyber	Mutant	Doomstopper
Super-Atomic	Neutronic	Vulcanoid
Mega-Buster	Android	Buzzernaut
Ultra	Telekinetic	Trashinator
Fatal	Phantom	Scorpio-Blaster
Radioactive	Invisible	Mantis Man
Mr Insecto	Magnetic	Shrink-O-Tron
The Amazing	Quantum	Invisobot
Shark-O-Matic	Ninja	Zeno-Flash

Superheroes

POSSIBLE SUPERPOWERS
(CHOOSE THREE)

X-ray vision

Invisibility

Supersonic hearing

Elasticity

Flying

Underwater breathing

Time warping

Mind control

Energy blasts

Superhuman speed

Superheroes

WHO IS YOUR SUPERHERO'S ARCHENEMY OR NEMESIS?

THE GARBAGE GREMLIN

SUPER-MOUSE

DOES YOUR SUPERHERO HAVE A HELPER OR SIDEKICK?

Superheroes

WHAT DOES YOUR SUPERHERO'S COSTUME LOOK LIKE?

POWER-CAPE

5 POWER-T

POWER PANTS

POWER-TRAINERS

JUDY MOODY'S SOCKS

WHAT IS YOUR SUPERHERO'S ONE WEAKNESS?

T Toad Pee Club

When Judy, Rocky and Frank form a club, Stink is dying to be a member. But he has to pick up a toad. When the toad pees on him, he becomes the newest member of the Toad Pee Club. *Eeuw!*

THESE FACTS ARE ALL TOADALLY TRUE!

★ Many toads have poison glands behind their eyes. If a toad is stressed, poison will ooze out of those glands.

DID YOU KNOW?

Frogs were hopping around during the Jurassic period. (That's about 190 million years ago.) Maybe that's why they have long jumping legs: they saved them from being some dinosaur's lunch!

★ American toads shed their skin every few weeks. The skin peels off in ONE PIECE. They collect it under their tongue and — GULP! — eat it.

★ IT'S RAINING TOADS!
It actually once rained toads in the town of Villa Angel Flores, Mexico. A small tornado picked up a bunch of toads from a nearby body of water and dropped them all over town. Motorists reported the amphibians falling from the sky at around 11 p.m.

Toad Pee Club

I'M KNOT KIDDING!
★ A group of toads is called a knot. A group of frogs is called an army.

PURPLE TOAD!
★ A new toad with neon-bright purple markings, the atelopus toad, was recently discovered in South America.

★ The most common toad you'll find in England is the bufo bufo.

★ The Goliath toad in Cameroon, West Africa, can grow to be as big as a house cat.

NO TOOTHBRUSH NEEDED!
★ Frogs have teeth, but toads do not.

DID YOU KNOW?

Some frogs can change colour according to changes in light, temperature, how wet it is outside, or even ... mood!

TRY THIS TRICKY TONGUE-TWISTER:
How many toes does Toady the toad have if a toad has ten toes total?

Toad Pee Club

TOAD TICKLERS!

WHERE DO BABY FROGS LEARN TO SWIM?

In a tadpool.

WHAT HAPPENS IF A FROG AND A TOAD BUMP INTO EACH OTHER?

They get tongue-tied.

WHAT DOES A TOAD ORDER IN A RESTAURANT?

French flies and a diet croak!

WHY ARE TOADS NORMALLY SO HAPPY?

Because they eat whatever bugs them.

Toilets

A word of advice from Stink:
Always look before you sit!

Wake up. Your toilet's ringing! It's not just dead goldfish that get flushed. Here's a list of some of the strangest stuff that has been flushed down the toilet:

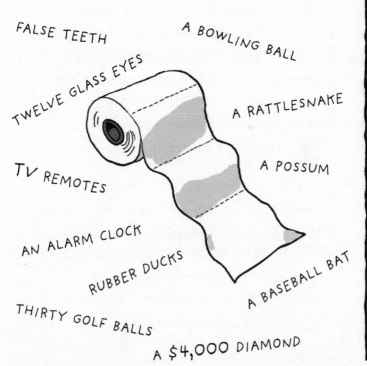

FALSE TEETH

A BOWLING BALL

TWELVE GLASS EYES

A RATTLESNAKE

A POSSUM

TV REMOTES

AN ALARM CLOCK

RUBBER DUCKS

A BASEBALL BAT

THIRTY GOLF BALLS

A $4,000 DIAMOND

DID YOU KNOW?

Every day in Europe, about 270,000 trees are flushed down the toilet in the form of toilet paper!

Toilets

★ **KEEP THE LID ON!**

More than just fake hands come out
of toilets. In one household an African
rock python rose up out of the toilet
bowl just as someone was about to sit
down! EEK!

★ **THE CORIOLIS FORCE**

Is that a name for the Northern
Lights? The title of a new **STAR WARS**
movie? Nope. The Coriolis force
explains why water goes down the
toilet clockwise in the northern
hemisphere and counterclockwise
in the southern hemesphere.

★ **WORLD'S BIGGEST MUSICAL TOILET?**

Chongqing, China, has opened a free,
four-storey public bathroom with
1,000 toilets, possibly the world's
largest. Here you can listen to
soothing music or watch TV while
you go about your business.

Toilets

★ **FAMOUS FIRSTS**

The first flush toilet is 3,700 years old. No lie. It was built in Greece, on the isle of Crete, for the queen.

★ **HEY, WHIZZ KID!**

Amsterdam is the proud home of a talking toilet. Creator Leonard van Munster has connected a public toilet to a computer. The toilet can ask you to lift the seat, warn you about germs or make fun of you if you don't wash your hands. It's a non-smoking toilet too. Light up and the toilet will actually start coughing and warn you about the hazards of smoking.

U Unbelievable ... or Not

Stink is the King of Fake Outs. Believe it ...
or not? Take this True *(Way)* or False
(No Way) Quiz to find out how easy it is
to fool you.

1. Masai warriors in Kenya spit at each
   other to say hello.

2. An asteroid bigger than an aircraft
   carrier hit Earth at the speed
   of 74,000 kilometres per hour on
   23 March 1989.

Unbelievable ... or Not

3. A mouse has more bones in its body than a human.

4. Donald Duck's middle name is Fattybottom.

5. Sir Thomas Overbury ate diamonds when he was locked up in the Tower of London for one hundred days.

Unbelievable ... or Not

6. The tornado sound in the film **TWISTER** was made by a moaning camel.

7. A mosquito has forty-seven teeth.

8. A man survived a great white shark attack by jamming his surfboard down the shark's throat.

Unbelievable ... or Not

9. In Pennsylvania, USA, 30,000 people have signed a petition to change Groundhog Day to Whistlepig Day.

10. Vexillology is the study of vampires.

11. An office chair with wheels will travel 8 kilometres a year.

(Turn to page 141 for the answers.)

Underwear

OK, let's face it. Underwear is just plain ... funny. Especially when your guinea pig gets into your clothes and ends up being chased around the room with tighty whities on his head!

★ **PANTS FOR THE AFTERLIFE**
Loincloths were the first underwear. King Tut was buried with 145 of them.

★ **RING IN THE NEW YEAR!**
In Italy wear red undies to ring in the new year. In Argentina wear pink.

★ **UNDERWEAR ELF**
In 2005 a teenager heard that one of the things poor people need most is underwear. She inspired people to donate 2,200 brand-new pairs of socks and undies to the Salvation Army.

★ **READ ALL ABOUT IT**
In the Middle Ages more people began wearing undies. As the undies wore out, the cloth was recycled to make paper. And the paper was used to make books.

DID YOU KNOW?

Since 2003, people in New York City have been celebrating National Underwear Day in early August.

V Ventriloquism

Ever since Stink saw a talking toilet brush on TV, he's wanted to make things talk without moving his lips.

◎ Ventriloquists make a dummy or puppet appear to talk by not moving their own lips as they speak.

◎ B, M and P are the hardest letters to make without your hips touching. Try it in a mirror. How do ventriloquists get around this? They replace B's with G's, turning "bottle" into "gottle".

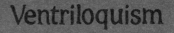

Ventriloquism

FAMOUS VENTRILOQUISTS AND THEIR DUMMIES

Edgar Bergen had Charlie McCarthy.
Shari Lewis had Lamb Chop.
Buffalo Bob Smith had Howdy Doody.
Fred Russell had Coster Joe.

OTHER DUMMIES
Knucklehead Smiff
Rodney Duckerfield
José Jalapeño
Mortimer Snerd

Virginia

My name is Stink and I come from …
Cuckoo?

Stink and Judy Moody live in the state
of Virginia in the USA. But the author,
Megan McDonald, had to think up a fake
name for their town. Here are some REAL
names of REAL towns in Virginia. No lie!

Antlers	Hurricane
Bagdad	Joe Neets
Ben Hur	Kermit
Bosses	Lick Skillet
Bumpass	Lipps
Butts	Moon
California	Moonlight
Clam	Mutt
Croaker	Needmore
Cuckoo	Nuttsville
Delaware	Ordinary
Eureka	Peach Bottom
Fries	Pocket
Frogtown	Short Pump
Goochland	Simplicity

MOODYVILLE?

What would you call Stink's hometown?
Here are some other real towns (and
their US state) to get you started:

Burnt Corn, ALABAMA
Chicken, ALASKA
Unalaska, ALASKA
Flippin, ARKANSAS
Wimp, CALIFORNIA
Chicken Head, FLORIDA
Two Egg, FLORIDA
Monkey's Eyebrow, KENTUCKY
Bald Head, MAINE
Boring, MARYLAND
Embarrass, MINNESOTA
Frankenstein, MISSOURI
Worms, NEBRASKA
Zap, NORTH DAKOTA
Worstville, OHIO
Ding Dong, TEXAS

W whisperers

Guinea pig whisperer (n.) a person, like Stink, who has a natural ability to understand and communicate with guinea pigs

There are many kinds of "whisperers" in the world.

★ Heather Mayers is an iguana whisperer. At the zoo in Syracuse, New York, USA, she coaxed Cy, a dying 152-centimetre-long iguana, back to health.

★ The first horse whisperer was Daniel Sullivan, an Irishman in the 1800s who could "gentle" the most out-of-control horses in a secret way, as if he spoke their language.

★ Ian Gordon is called a shark whisperer. He's been swimming with great whites for almost thirty years.

★ Cindy Wegner of Hershey, Pennsylvania, USA, gets paid to talk to praying mantises. She's an animal communicator, someone who claims to know what animals are thinking and feeling.

Whisperers

HERE ARE A FEW HELPFUL FACTS FOR THE WOULD-BE WHISPERER:

- Chimps say hello by touching hands.
- Elephants show affection by entwining trunks.
- Gorillas stick out their tongues when angry.
- Horses rub noses.

Who's Who?

Mum
*Stink's mum.
Knows a thing or two
about toilet water.*

Judy
*Big sister.
The mudiest of all.*

Webster
*(NOT the dictionary.)
Best friend.*

Sophie
*(Real name, Elizabeth.)
Other best friend.*

Who's Who?

Stink
Star of the show.
Super sniffer.

Mrs Dempster
Stink's second grade teacher.
Queen of Pyjama Day.

coming soon...

Dad
Stink's dad.
The Piñata Papa.

Mrs Birdwistle
Owner of Fur & Fangs.
Guinea pig heroine.

X X Marks the Spot

What does *x* have to do with Stink?
Not much. But what's an encyclopedia
without it? Guess which *x* words are real
words. Hey! No peeking at the dictionary!

xantaphon (n.) a rare hummingbird from
  Xanto, China

xebec (n.) a small ship with three masts

xenatrog (n.) a rare desert amphibian

xenolith (n.) a piece of rock embedded in
  another rock

Xenon (n.) a planet formed by kryptonite
  in Superman comics

xenotech (n.) a computer expert in
  xeno-transporting

X Marks the Spot

xerocitis: (n.) an inability to remember the number zero brought on by brain-freeze

xeroderma (n.) a disease that turns the skin flaky like fish scales

xeromorphic (n.) a name for plants specially adapted to survive in the desert

X-ray star (n.) a star in the heavens that emits radioactive rays

xycron (n.) a unit of measure that equals 100 cronos

xylomatic (n.) a robotic xylophone that plays up to three hundred tunes automatically

(Turn to page 141 for the answers.)

Y Yeti (Y not? What else is there?)

The yeti is a giant hairy creature rumoured to live in the Himalayas. It's also known as the Abominable Snowman, Sasquatch or Bigfoot.

★ In 1961 Nepal declared that the yeti did exist and adopted it as their national symbol. They even honoured the yeti on a postage stamp.

★ A yeti cousin might be a yowie. A yowie is a hairy, gorilla-like cross between a lizard and an ant. Also called a bunyip.

Yeti

REMARKABLE YETI QUALITIES

★ whistles and growls or roars like a lion

★ tosses huge stones as if they were pebbles

★ can kill with a single punch

★ stands between 213 and 305 centimetres tall

★ has reddish hair and a terrible smell

Z Zero

$$5 \times 0 = 0$$

Stink is really good at maths. Actually, he's really good at just about everything to do with school. In honour of Stink's big brain, meet the number zero!

Million has 6 zeros
Billion has 9 zeros

$$9 \times 0 = 0$$

Trillion has 12 zeros
Quadrillion has 15 zeros
Septillion has 24 zeros
Nonillion has 30 zeros
Decillion has 33 zeros

$$0 \times 0 = 0$$

Undecillion has 36 zeros
Duodecillion has 39 zeros
Quattuordecillion has 45 zeros
Octodecillion has 57 zeros
Novemdecillion has 60 zeros
Centillion has 303 zeros

$$11 \times 0 = 0$$

$4 \times 0 = 0$

The word **googol**, a number with 100 zeros, was thought up in 1920 by a nine-year-old.

100,000,000,000,000,000,000,000,
000,000,000,000,000,000,000,
000,000,000,000,000,000,000,
000,000,000,000,000,000,000,
000,00

$7 \times 0 = 0$

Oops!
The Web search engine Google was named after this number, but it was accidentally misspelled.

A googolplex is not a cinema with a hundred screens. It's the number 1 followed by a googol of zeros.

$8 \times 0 = 0$

Zzzzz's

COUNTING ZZZ'S

Stink was catching some zzz's on the bus one day when he missed his stop.

Check out these other sleep-related facts:

AMAZZZING!

◎ People have been known to take catnaps with their eyes open. (Maybe they should be called fishnaps, since fish always sleep with their eyes open.)

◎ Ducks afraid of being preyed upon sleep by keeping one-half of their brain awake while the other half sleeps. Dolphins are half-brainers too!

DID YOU KNOW?

The record for staying awake is 18 days, 21 hours and 40 minutes, during a rocking-chair marathon.

Zzzzz's

◎ Teenagers need as much sleep as babies and small children.

◎ Counting sheep actually does help people fall asleep. Counting toads or guinea pigs works just fine too. But guess what? Imagining a waterfall or beach will make you fall asleep even faster!

◎ It's the law! In Oklahoma, USA, it's against the law to sleep on a refrigerator that's outdoors.

◎ In the US state of Alaska, it's against the law to wake up a sleeping bear to take its picture.

DID YOU KNOW?

If you are Stink's age, you have already spent 851 days, or 2.3 years, of your life sleeping.

THE SLEEPYHEAD AWARD
GOES TO...

BATS! Brown bats sleep
20 hours a day.

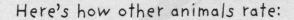

Here's how other animals rate:

Python	18 hours
Tiger	16 hours
Hamster	14 hours
Cat	12 hours
Pig	8 hours
Cow	4 hours
Horse	3 hours
African elephant	3 hours

The ostrich sleeps for only 15
minutes at a time!

Wondering which books inspired the entries in *Stink-O-Pedia*? Take a look! How many of them have *you* read?

Stink: The Incredible Shrinking Kid

Anatomy of Stink
Backpack Backbreakers
Best Friends
Comics
Fur & Fangs
Madison, James
Newts
Optical Illusions
Q & A
Short, Shorter, Shortest!
Slime
Superheroes

Stink and the Incredible Super-Galactic Jawbreaker

Backpack Backbreakers
Candyland
Glow in the Dark
Idiom
Jawbreakers
Letters and Letter Writing
Q & A

Stink and the World's Worst Super-Stinky Sneakers

Anatomy of Stink
Backpack Backbreakers
Best Friends
Corpse Flower

Eu-REEK-a!
Inventions
James
Museums
Nose
Professional Smeller
Q & A
Slime

Stink and the Great Guinea Pig Express

Astro (or Astro-NOT)
Duct Tape
Fur & Fangs
Guinea Pig Mania
Hugh Mongous and
   Other Huge Stuff
Museums
Rescue Me!
Rodents
Underwear
Whisperers

Judy Moody

Fur & Fangs
Ka-Ching!
Moon Rocks
Practical Jokes
Toad Pee Club
Toilets
Virginia

And look for these other Stink-y topics in forthcoming books about Stink E. Moody:

Karate
Pluto
Ventriloquism
Yeti

Selected Sources

Books:

The Bathroom Readers' Institute, *Uncle John's Strange and Scary Bathroom Reader for Kids Only!*, Ashland, OR: Bathroom Readers' Press, 2006

Branzei, Sylvia, *Grossology*, illustrated by Jack Keely, New York: Price Stern Sloan, 2002

Buckley, James, and Robert Stremme, *Scholastic Book of Lists, New and Updated*, New York: Scholastic Reference, 2006

Glenday, Craig (ed.), *Guinness World Records 2007*, New York: Bantam Books, 2007

Janeczko, Paul B., *Top Secret: A Handbook of Codes, Ciphers, and Secret Writing*, illustrated by Jenna LaReau, Cambridge, MA: Candlewick Press, 2004

Johnson, Anne Akers, *The Buck Book*, Palo Alto, CA: Klutz, 1993

Jones, Charlotte Foltz, *Accidents May Happen*, illustrated by John O'Brien, New York: Delacorte Press, 1996

———, *Mistakes That Worked*, illustrated by John O'Brien, New York: Doubleday, 1991

Joyce, C. Alan (ed.), *The World Almanac for Kids 2008*, Mahwah, NJ: World Almanac Books, 2008

Masoff, Joy, *Oh, Yikes! History's Grossest, Wackiest Moments*, illustrated by Terry Sirrell, New York: Workman Publishing, 2006

———, *Oh Yuck! The Encyclopedia of Everything Nasty*, illustrated by Terry Sirrell, New York: Workman Publishing, 2000

Mooney, Julie, and the editors of Ripley's Believe It or Not!, *The World of Ripley's Believe It or Not!*, New York: Black Dog and Leventhal, 1999

Morgan, Matthew, and Samantha Barnes, *Children's Miscellany Too: More Useless Information That's Essential to Know*, illustrated by Niki Catlow, San Francisco: Chronicle Books, 2006

Rowen, Beth, *Time for Kids Almanac 2008*, New York: Time for Kids Books, 2008

Selected Sources

Stillman, Janice (ed.), *The Old Farmer's Almanac for Kids*, Dublin, NH: Yankee Publishing, 2005

Swain, Ruth Freeman, *How Sweet It Is (and Was): The History of Candy*, illustrated by John O'Brien, New York: Holiday House, 2003

Szpirglas, Jeff, *They Did What?! Your Guide to Weird and Wacky Things People Do*, illustrated by Dave Whamond, Toronto: Maple Tree Press, 2005

Taplin, Sam, and Stephen Wright, *The Usborne Official Pirate's Handbook*, illustrated by Ian McNee, Tulsa, OK: Usborne Books, 2007

Terban, Marvin, *Scholastic Dictionary of Idioms*, New York: Scholastic, 1996

Tucker, Tom, *Brainstorm! The Stories of Twenty American Kid Inventors*, illustrated by Richard Loehle, New York: Farrar, Straus and Giroux, 1995

Wulffson, Don L., *The Kid Who Invented the Popsicle: And Other Surprising Stories About Inventions*, New York: Cobblehill Books, 1997

Websites:

Bentley Snow Crystal Collection of the Buffalo Museum of Science, "Primary Collection", www.bentley.sciencebuff.org/collection.asp (accessed 11 June 2008)

The Duct Tape Guys, "The Ultimate Books on Tape", www.ducttapeguys.com (accessed 11 June 2008)

Graham's Paddock, "The Incredible World of Navel Fluff Part 1: The Collection", www.feargod.net/fluff.html (accessed 11 June 2008)

National Confectioners Association, www.ecandy.com (accessed 11 June 2008)

Smithfield and Isle of Wight Convention and Visitors Bureau, "Attractions", www.smithfield-virginia.com/attractions.html (accessed 11 June 2008)

Space Mart, "World's Forests Being Flushed Down the Toilet", www.spacemart. com/reports/Worlds_Forests_Being_Flushed_Down_The_Toilet.html (accessed 11 June 2008)

Answers

p. 22: Encyclopedia

The twenty spelling mistakes in this book can be found on these pages:

5	*genious* should be *genius*
10	*starrs* should be *stars*
22	*Purfickt* should be *Perfect*
25	*drane* should be *drain*
29	*lite* should be *light*
36	*witch* should be *which*
43	*rite* should be *write*
49	*YU* should be *YOU*
50	*trubble* should be *trouble*
57	*roks* should be *rocks*
68	*see* should be *sea*
72	*trosers* should be *trousers*
78	*freee* should be *free*
85	*wait* should be *weight*
92	*faller* should be *taller*
95	*nostrilz* should be *nostrils*
97	*bown* should be *down*
108	*hemesphere* should be *hemisphere*
116	*hips* should be *lips*
122	*mudiest* should be *moodiest*

p. 33: Hic!

All of them!

pp. 39–41: Idiom

1. D   Feeling like a heel.
2. A   Making a mountain out of a molehill.
3. C   Costing an arm and a leg.
4. E   As cute as a bug's ear.
5. B   Sour grapes.

Answers

p. 55: Madison, James
If Stink is 112 centimetres tall and James Madison is 163 centimetres tall, then Stink is 51 centimetres (163 cm − 112 cm = 51) shorter than James Madison.

p. 57: Moon Rocks
The mineral armalcolite was named for Neil **Arm**strong, Buzz **Al**drin and Michael **Col**lins.

pp. 64–65: Optical Illusions
The staggered black and white stripes are exactly the same width from end to end.

The vertical black and white stripes are perfectly parallel, perfectly straight.

The dot in the centre of the flower on the right is bigger than the dot in the centre of the flower on the left.

pp. 78–79: Q&A
1. 21,280.
2. The Golden Clothes Peg Award.
3. *Skeletons in My Closet!*
4. Kimo.
5. Jack Frost.
6. Number 4, because James Madison was the fourth president.
7. He has Skeleton-itis, Fear-of-Skeletons disease.
8. Smithfield, home of the World's Biggest Ham.
★ Super-Intelligent All-Time Bonus Question: Fang.

p. 87: Secret Codes
Skinks Rule

Answers

p. 89: Secret Codes
You smell like a corpse flower

pp. 110–113: Unbelievable ... or Not
1. **Way!** Masai warriors often spit as a greeting!
2. **No way!** The asteroid missed Earth by about six hours.
3. **Way!** A human adult has 206 bones. A mouse has more than 350 – as many as an elephant!
4. **No way!** His middle name is Fauntleroy.
5. **Way!** He was poisoned with nitric acid, hemlock and ground-up diamonds.
6. **Way!** The sound of the camel's moan was slowed down and used as the sound of the tornado.
7. **Way!** The teeth are used to cut into the skin and produce an increased blood flow.
8. **Way!** It happened in 1991.
9. **No way!** But *whistlepig* is another name for groundhog.
10. **No way!** Vexillology is the study of flags.
11. **No way!** It actually travels MORE – about 11–12 kilometres per year!

pp. 124–125: X Marks the Spot
The real words are: xebec, xenolith, Xenon, xeroderma, xeromorphic, X-ray star.

First published 2009 by Walker Books Ltd
87 Vauxhall Walk, London SE11 5HJ

8 10 9 7

Text © 2009 Megan McDonald
Illustrations © 2009 Peter H. Reynolds

Text excerpts from:
Judy Moody © 2000 Megan McDonald; *Doctor Judy Moody* © 2004 Megan McDonald
(now available as *Judy Moody: The Doctor Is In!*); *Stink: The Incredible Shrinking Kid* © 2005
Megan McDonald; *Stink and the Incredible Super-Galactic Jawbreaker* © 2006 Megan McDonald;
Stink and the World's Worst Super-Stinky Sneakers © 2007 Megan McDonald; *Stink and the Great
Guinea Pig Express* © 2008 Megan McDonald

Illustrations from:
Stink: The Incredible Shrinking Kid © 2005 Peter H. Reynolds; *Stink and the Incredible Super-Galactic
Jawbreaker* © 2006 Peter H. Reynolds; *Stink and the World's Worst Super-Stinky Sneakers* © 2007
Peter H. Reynolds; *Judy Moody & Stink: The Holly Joliday* © 2007 Peter H. Reynolds; *Stink and
the Great Guinea Pig Express* © 2008 Peter H. Reynolds; *Judy Moody & Stink: The Mad, Mad, Mad,
Mad Treasure Hunt* © 2009 Peter H. Reynolds

The right of Megan McDonald and Peter H. Reynolds to be identified as
author and illustrator respectively of this work has been asserted by them
in accordance with the Copyright, Designs and Patents Act 1988

This book has been typeset in Stone Informal

Printed and bound in Great Britain by Clays Ltd, St Ives plc

British Library Cataloguing in Publication Data:
a catalogue record for this book is available from the British Library

ISBN 978-1-4063-2436-5

www.walker.co.uk

CHECK IT OUT!

I have my own place
in cyberspace.

Come and visit!

www.stinkmoody.com